John Albert Monroe

The Rhode Island Artillery at the First Battle of Bull Run

John Albert Monroe

The Rhode Island Artillery at the First Battle of Bull Run

ISBN/EAN: 9783744732284

Printed in Europe, USA, Canada, Australia, Japan

Cover: Foto ©ninafisch / pixelio.de

More available books at **www.hansebooks.com**

PERSONAL NARRATIVES

OF THE

BATTLES OF THE REBELLION,

BEING

PAPERS READ BEFORE THE

RHODE ISLAND SOLDIERS AND SAILORS

HISTORICAL SOCIETY.

No. 2.

" Quaeque ipse miserrima vidi,
Et quorum pars magna fui."

PROVIDENCE:
SIDNEY S. RIDER.
1878.

PRINTED BY PROVIDENCE PRESS COMPANY.

THE RHODE ISLAND ARTILLERY

AT THE

FIRST BATTLE OF BULL RUN.

BY

J. ALBERT MONROE,

(Late Lieutenant-Colonel First Rhode Island Light Artillery.)

———◆———

PROVIDENCE:
SIDNEY S. RIDER.
1878.

THE RHODE ISLAND ARTILLERY

AT THE

FIRST BATTLE OF BULL RUN.

———◆———

WHEN the first call for troops, to serve for the term of three months, was made by President Lincoln, in 1861, for the purpose of suppressing the rebellion, which had assumed most dangerous proportions to the National Government, the Marine Artillery, of this city, responded cheerfully to the call, and under the command of Captain Charles H. Tompkins, left Providence, April eighteenth, for the seat of war.

The senior officer of the company, who remained at home, was Captain William H. Parkhurst, then book-keeper at the Mechanics Bank on South Main Street. Before the company was fairly away, I called upon him and suggested the propriety of call-

ing a meeting to organize a new company to take
the place of the one that had gone. The suggestion
met his views, and he at once published a notice that
a meeting for the purpose would be held that evening at the armory of the Marines, on Benefit Street.
The meeting was largely attended, and comprised
among its numbers a great many of our most intel-
ligent and influential citizens. A large number of
names were enrolled that night as members of the
new company, and arrangements were made to have
the armory open daily, for the purpose of obtaining
additional signatures to the roll of membership. In
a few days some three hundred names were obtained,
and every man whose name was enrolled seemed
to take the greatest interest in having the work
proceed.

By general consent, rather than by appointment
or election, I assumed the duty of conducting the
drills and of reducing matters to a system. It was
supposed at the time that the force already called
into the field, consisting of seventy-five thousand
men, would be amply sufficient to effectually quell
the disturbance that had arisen at the South, but

there appeared to be in the minds of all the men who gathered at the Marines' Armory, a quiet determination to go to the assistance of those who had already gone, should they appear to need aid. The call for men to serve for the period of three years put a new phase upon matters. Those whose private business was of such importance that absence from home that length of time would injure the interests of others as well as their own, withdrew, leaving more than a sufficient number to man a full battery. From that time drilling of the men proceeded uninterruptedly both day and night. A greater number than the capacity of the armory would admit of drilling at one time, presented themselves daily. Many of the evenings were spent in taking the men out on the streets and to vacant lots near by, exercising them in marching drill. Through the influence of Governor Sprague the company was furnished with a complete battery of twelve pounder James guns, which arrived here some time in May, I think, and then the drills became spirited in exercise in the manual of the piece, mechanical manœuvres, as well as in marching.

About the first of June Lieutenant William H.
Reynolds and First Sergeant Thomas F. Vaughn of
the three months battery, were appointed Captain
and First Lieutenant respectively, and J. Albert
Monroe, John A. Tompkins and William B. Weeden
were appointed Second, Third and Fourth Lieutenants, and they were so commissioned. The com-
missions should have been one captain, two first
lieutenants and two second lieutenants, but there
was so little knowledge of just the right way to do
things at that time, that this error occurred, and it
was not until after the First Battle of Bull Run that
it was corrected.

On the sixth of June, 1861, the company was
mustered into the United States service by Colonel
S. Loomis of the United States Army, for the period
of " three years unless sooner discharged," in a large
room of a building on Eddy street.

On the eighth of June, the regular business of soldier's life began by the company going into camp on
Dexter Training Ground. The time was occupied in
detachment and battery drills until the nineteenth of
the month, when the guns, carriages, and the horses

also, if my memory serves me, were embarked on the steamer Kill-von-Kull, at the Fox Point wharf. The steamer landed at Elizabethport, New Jersey, where the battery and men were transferred to cars. The train left Elizabethport about four o'clock in the afternoon. The journey to Washington was a most tedious one. Harrisburg was not reached until the next morning, and it was not until the following morning that the train arrived in Washington.

Although the journey was a long one, and tiresome, many incidents transpired to relieve the tedium of the trip. At Baltimore, which was passed through in the evening, every man was on the *qui vive*, with nerves strung to the tension, so great was the fear that an attack might be made upon us. Every one who had a revolver carried it cocked. A corporal, who is now a commissioned officer in the regular army, remarked to me that he never was in such danger in his life, though nothing had occurred to awaken a sense of danger, except that a small pebble was thrown, probably by some boys, that hit one of the gun carriages on the flat car, upon which he and I were riding. The next day rebel flags, in imagination, were frequently discovered while passing through Maryland.

On our arrival at Washington, the morning of the twenty-second, we were cordially greeted by Captain Tompkins of the three months battery, and he and his men lent us every assistance in their power. The company went into camp in Gale's woods, with the Second Regiment Rhode Island Infantry, and adjoining were the camps of the three months organizations—the First Regiment Rhode Island Detached Militia and the First Battery. The ground occupied by the three months men was already known as "Camp Sprague;" the ground occupied by the Second Battery and the Second Regiment was named "Camp Clark," in honor of Bishop Thomas M. Clark, who had taken a great interest in the raising and the organization of troops in Rhode Island.

Affairs went along more smoothly than could reasonably have been expected from men just taken from the pursuits of civil life. Captain Reynolds, with rare tact, won the confidence of all his men and officers. Section and battery drills took place daily, in the morning, and the afternoons were generally spent at standing gun drill.

On the ninth of July, while at section drill, a sad accident occurred, by which Corporal Morse (Nathan T.) and private Bourne (William E.) lost their lives, and private Freeman (Edward R.) was very seriously injured. From some unaccountable cause the limber chest upon which they were mounted exploded, almost instantly killing Morse and Bourne and severely injuring Freeman. The remains of Morse and Bourne were escorted to the depot by the company, and there was extended to them a marked tribute of respect upon their arrival and burial at home.

On the sixteenth of July the battery left Camp Clark at half past one o'clock in the morning, with the First and Second Rhode Island Regiments, but it was broad daylight before the command got fairly away from the vicinity of the camp. Under the lead of Colonel Ambrose E. Burnside, who had command of the Second New Hampshire, Seventy-first New York, First and Second Rhode Island Regiments and the battery, as a brigade, the company marched over

Long Bridge to a point about ten miles from Washington, where the whole brigade bivouacked for the night. The next morning the march was resumed at day-break, and Fairfax Court House was reached about half past one in the afternoon. The battery was parked and the company went into camp near the Court House, on the ground and near the residence of a Mr. Stephenson, an English gentleman with a large and interesting family, every member of which appeared to do their utmost to promote our comfort. Early the next morning, Thursday the eighteenth, the advance again began and continued with numerous delays until near night-fall, when camp was established near Centreville, on the plantation of a Mr. Utteback.

On the morning of Sunday the twenty-first the brigade broke camp and commenced the march towards Manassas. The march was a tedious and lonely one until daybreak. The morning broke as clear and lovely as any that ever opened upon Virginia soil. In the early daylight it seemed to dawn upon the minds of both officers and men, that they were there for a fixed purpose, and that the actual

THE FIRST BATTLE OF BULL RUN.

business of their vocation was to commence. Previously, nearly all had thought that upon the approach of the United States troops, with their splendid equipment and the vast resources behind them, the "rebel mob," as it was deemed, but which we afterwards learned to respect as the rebel forces, would flee from their position and disperse.

General Hunter's column, to which Colonel Burnside's brigade was attached, was the right of the advancing line, and soon after sunrise the report of heavy guns to the left told us that the work of the day had commenced. Steadily, however, the column pushed on, but with frequent halts, until Sudley Church was reached, where a short stop was made in the shade of the thick foliage of the trees in the vicinity of the church. The battery was following the Second Rhode Island, a portion of which were deployed as skirmishers, and contrary to the custom of throwing them, the skirmishers, well in advance, they moved directly on the flanks of the column. Suddenly the outposts of the enemy opened fire, which, to our inexperienced ears, sounded like the explosion

2

of several bunches of fire crackers. Immediately after came the order. "FORWARD YOUR BATTERY!" Although the order was distinctly heard by both officers and men of the battery. I have never believed that it was definitely known whether it was given by General McDowell or General Hunter. With most commendable promptness, but without that caution which a battery commander learns to observe only by experience. Captain Reynolds rushed his battery forward at once at a sharp gallop. The road at this point was skirted by woods, but a short distance beyond, the battery emerged upon an open field, and at once went into position and opened fire.

The battery was now considerably in advance of the infantry and could easily have been captured and taken from the field by the enemy, before the supporting infantry were formed in line of battle; and two years later under the same circumstances, the entire battery would have been lost; but neither side hardly understood the rudiments of the art of war. When we reached the open field the air seemed to be filled with myriads of serpents, such was the sound of the bullets passing through it. Above us and around us on every side, they seemed to be hissing, writhing and twisting. I have been under many a hot fire, but I don't think that, in nearly four years experience, I ever heard so many bullets in such a short space of time. Suddenly thrown into a position, the realities of which had been only feebly imagined and underestimated, it is surprising that all did so well. I remember the first thing that came into my mind was the wish that I was at home out of danger's way, and immediately following came the sense of my obligation to perform every duty of the position that I filled. The same spirit seemed to animate every one of the battery, and each and every one worked manfully throughout the day.

Hardly had we arrived on the field, when with almost the rapidity of lightning it passed from one to another that Sergeant George L. Randolph was wounded. He was a great favorite with the entire company, his personal qualities being such as to win the respect and love of all. Although every one felt that a dark cloud had thrown its shadow over us, still there was no faltering. Captain Reynolds, who had marked affection for Sergeant Randolph, sacrificed the impulses of his nature and stuck to his command to look out for the interests of all.

A great many amusing incidents occurred during the first hour of the action, that, undoubtedly, have afforded many hours of enjoyment to the partakers. Two of the corporals seemed to find great relief in getting behind a limber-chest with its cover opened, though they pluckily performed their duties, and I confess that I experienced a similar relief myself when I was obliged to go there once or twice to examine the ammunition, though I fully realized that it was like a quail running his head into a snowbank to escape the hunter.

The firing was exceedingly rapid, every one appearing to feel that the great object was to make as much noise as possible, and get an immense quantity of iron into the enemy's line in the shortest possible space of time, without regard to whether it hit anything or not. The firing was principally directed towards the smoke of a rebel battery, posted near what is shown as the "Henry House" on the map accompanying General McDowell's report of the action, but was really the "Lewis House,"

which house served as the headquarters of General
Beauregard. But very little attention was paid to the
effect of the shot for some time. Considerable of the
fire was directed into a clump of woods in our imme-
diate front, in which was quite a force of rebel infantry, and I have reason to believe that this fire was
very effective; for, upon visiting the spot during
the action of the Second Bull Run I found the trees
thickly scarred at the height where the shot would
be likely to do the most execution.

We had with us a young man, who was hardly
more than a mere boy, by the name of Henry H.
Stewart, who had been taken out from here by Captain Reynolds to act as an orderly and guidon, who,
while nearly every one else was excited and every-
thing was in confusion, preserved, apparently, the
utmost coolness, moving from point to point as
calmly as if performing the ordinary duties of
parade, and it was not until I ordered him so to do
that he dismounted from his horse. But the coolest
one of our number, and, I believe, the coolest man
on the field that day, was Sergeant G. Lyman
Dwight. When the storm of bullets was thickest

and the rebel artillery was delivering upon us its
heaviest fire, Dwight would step aside from the
smoke from his gun, and seemed perfectly absorbed
by the sublime and magnificent spectacle. Once or
twice he called my attention to the glorious scene,
but I was too much engaged and my mind was too
much occupied in thinking how we were to get out
of the "glorious scene" to take much pleasure in
the observance of it. Dwight was associated with
me, more or less, during the whole war, and I found
in his character more admirable qualities than I ever
found possessed by any other man, and the objec-
tionable qualities of his nature I could never dis-
cover. War had no terrors for him, and his æsthetic
taste found beauties to admire even under the most
adverse circumstances. When the leaden rain and
iron hail were thickest, I have known him to muse
upon philosophy, and to repeat a quotation from
some favorite author applicable to the situation and
circumstances. He was quick and unerring, and no
emergency could arise that would deprive him of
his full self-possession. This is digressing from my
subject, but my admiration for him was such, that I

feel justified in thus alluding to a life that was prac-
tically lost in the war, though his death did not take
place until within the past year.

About one or two hours after the engagement
began, Captain Reynolds, with Lieutenants Tompkins and Weeden, went off to the right of our position with two guns, which were placed in position
near the Doogan House, I think, where they went
earnestly at work. During their absence, Sergeant
John H. Hammond, of my section, reported to me
that he was entirely out of ammunition, and as I knew
that there was no reserve supply for the James gun
within available distance, I directed him to take his
piece to the rear, to some safe place and wait for
orders. I remained with my other piece and the
pieces of Lieutenant Vaughn. Either before or after
this, a shot from the enemy struck the axle of one
of the pieces, which entirely disabled it.* The gun

---

* At the conclusion of the reading of this paper, Governor Sprague and
William A. Sabin, formerly a member of the battery, gave it as their recollection that the stock of the gun carriage broke on account of the extreme eleva-
tion of the gun, and that it was not hit by the enemy's shot; but a letter of
mine, written after the battle, implies that the gun carriage was struck by a
shot.

was dismounted and slung under its limber and immediately taken from the field. The mechanical maneuvres that the men had been exercised in before they left home, for the first time now found opportunity for practical application, and the slinging of the piece was performed as thoroughly as upon the floor of the drill-room.

Sometime after mid-day Governor Sprague, accompanied by Captain Reynolds, rode up to me and said, "Monroe, can't you get your guns over on the hill there, where those batteries are?" The batteries referred to were those of Captains Ricketts and Griffin, which were then in position near the "Henry" or "Lewis" House. Without any thought, except to take the pieces to that position, I ordered my remaining piece and one of Lieutenant Vaughn's forward, and accompanied by Captain Reynolds proceeded across the turnpike and up the road leading to the place where the two batteries were in position. The day was a very hot one, and I remember that my thirst, at this time, was almost unendurable. Crossing the turnpike, I saw a pool of muddy water which appeared like the watering places beside our

New England country roads, where they are crossed
by rivulets or brooks. Although the water was
muddy and the dead bodies of a man and a horse
were lying in it, so great was my thirst, I could not
resist the inclination to dismount to slake it, and did
so. Quickly remounting, I went forward with the
section through what appeared to be a lane, on a
side hill, which was completely filled with infantry,
who had been hotly engaged in the fight since the
opening of the battle. Just as we diverged to the right
in order to secure the ground between the two batteries, a shot came very near to me, and turning my
head, I saw Captain Reynolds go off his horse. I
supposed, of course, that he was hit, and started to
his assistance, but to my surprise he jumped up
nimbly and remounted, saying, "That about took my
breath away." The shot must have passed within a
few inches of him, and was what afterwards was
known in soldier's parlance, as "a close call."

We pushed forward and got the pieces in position
between Ricketts's and Griffin's batteries, but before
a single shot could be fired, the fatal mistake of the
day occurred, the mistake of supposing a rebel com-

mand to be a portion of our own forces. Thick and
fast their bullets came in upon us, and they were
fast approaching in their charge, when with almost
superhuman energy, and with a rapidity that I never
saw excelled and I think I never saw equaled, our
cannoneers limbered to the rear and we withdrew
with a loss in material of only a caisson, the pole of
which was broken in the endeavor to turn on the
side hill, and there was no time then to stop for
repairs. Here private Bubb (Frederick) lost his
life, and private Vose (Warren L.) was wounded and
taken prisoner. A bullet went through my cap and
ploughed a little furrow in my scalp. Jumping
from my horse to assist Sergeant Wilcox (G.
Holmes) in limbering his piece, the animal dashed
off frightened by the confusion, and I was obliged to
ride to the rear on the stock of the gun carriage.

Arriving on the northerly side of the turnpike, we
were joined by Captain Reynolds near the "Doogan"
House, and shortly after by Lieutenant Weeden.
Captain Reynolds said that he had just seen Arnold,
(Captain of the regular artillery) who had lost his
battery. I hastened with the two guns off to the

left, to the position that we first occupied in the morning, and, going into battery, commenced firing. The men worked steadier and cooler than they had at any time during the day. All at once there emerged from the timber in our front, a regiment or brigade of the enemy, evidently preparing for a charge upon us, and simultaneously came an order, from Captain Reynolds, I believe, to limber to the rear. I could not resist the temptation, in spite of the order, to give them one more shot before parting, and I directed the left piece to be loaded with canister. As the piece was fired, the enemy, apparently, was just ready to move forward on their charge. It appeared to me that a gap of full twenty feet was made in their line, which completely staggered them. This, I think, was the last shot fired on the field that day. The first one was fired by Sergeant Dwight.

Leaving the field on foot with this piece, I found the remainder of the battery a short distance away on the road, moving toward Centreville. Procuring a horse from one of the sergeants, I returned to the field in search of the horse that I had lost, for which

I had great affection. The scene was one of inde-
scribable confusion, although there appeared to be
no fright or terror in the minds of the men who
were leaving the field. Officers seemed to have lost
all identity with their commands, subalterns and
even colonels moving along in the scattered crowd
as if their work was over and they were wearily
seeking the repose of their domiciles. The scene
was such as to remind one of that which can be seen
daily in any large manufacturing town or village,
when the operatives, let loose by the expiration of
their hours of labor, all set out for their respective
homes. During working hours the system for work
is maintained, but upon the ringing of the bell, all
depart according to their respective bents and wills.
So upon this field, the general impression seemed to
be that the day's work was done and that the next
thing in order was repose. There were a few notable
exceptions. I remember well a large and powerful
man, a field officer of what I took to be a Maine
regiment—at any rate he and his men were uniformed
in gray—using the most strenuous exertions to get
his men together. He coaxed, threatened and

applied to them every epithet that he seemed capable of, but all to no purpose. The idea of the men seemed to be that their work was over for the day, and that they were going home to rest, not realizing apparently, that whether on or off duty, they were subject to the orders that their officers deemed best to give.

The bullets began to whistle uncomfortably thick, and I gave up the search for my horse, and rejoined the battery, then moving along the road in good order, in which condition it continued until the head of the column reached the foot of the hill at the base of which flowed what is known as Cub Run. Here was a bridge rendered impassable by the wrecks of several baggage wagons. In the ford at the left was an overturned siege gun, completely blocking up that passage, and the right ford was completely filled with troops and wagons. Of course the leading team of the battery had to halt, and it was impossible to stop the rear carriages on the steep hill, so that the column became only a jumbled heap of horses, limbers, caissons and gun carriages. To add to the confusion, just at this moment a rebel

3

battery in our rear opened fire, and it seemed as if every one of their shots came down into our very midst. The men immediately set to work taking the horses from their harnesses, after doing which they mounted upon them in the most lively manner. Some horses carried only a single passenger, others had on their backs doublets and some triplets. Still, notwithstanding all this confusion, there did not seem to me to be what has been almost universally reported, "a perfect panic." It appeared to me only that confusion which of necessity must arise from the sudden breaking up of organization.

I forded the run on the right hand, or down stream side of the bridge. Going up the hill after crossing, I overtook Captain Reynolds who crossed a little in advance of me, and just as I rode along side of him, a shot from the enemy's artillery struck the ground only a few feet from us. Unsophisticated as I was, I could not understand why they should continue to fire upon us when we were doing the best that we could to let them alone, and I said to Captain Reynolds, " What do you suppose they are trying to do?" His reply was a characteristic one : "They are trying to kill every mother's son of us; that is what they are trying to do," the truth of which was very forcibly impressed upon me as shot after shot came screeching after us in rapid succession.

After getting beyond range of their fire, each one exerted himself to get together as many members of the battery as possible, and upon reaching Centreville all who had collected together assembled at the house of Mr. Utteback, which we had left in the morning. Captain Reynolds and most of the others, took up their quarters on the stoop or piazza of the house. I was suffering severely from a lame leg, which had been injured during the action by the recoil of a piece, and having won the good graces of the family during our stay there, I asked for more comfortable quarters, and was given a nice bed. About two o'clock in the morning, I was awakened and informed that orders had been received to leave for Washington at once. While I was dressing, one of the daughters of Mr. Utteback slipped into the room with a flask of wine which she handed to me with the remark, "I think you may need this before you reach Washington," and she added, "Don't, for

Heaven's sake, tell anybody of it." The act was an extremely kind one, for from the moment of our arrival on the farm, every member of the family had been besieged for liquor of any kind, but they had persistently refused to furnish any, declaring that they had not a drop in the house. I concealed the flask under my vest and found its contents of great cheer and comfort during our long night ride.

Upon going out of the house to resume the march, I found, to my surprise, that some time during the night, private Scott (Charles V.) had arrived in camp with the piece that I had sent off the field under Sergeant Hammond for want of ammunition. Upon enquiring of Scott for the particulars of his becoming possessed of it, he informed me that he got strayed from the company, and while picking his way through the woods, came upon the piece with all or a portion of the horses still hitched to it. Calling upon some infantry men near by, who were also estray, he mounted one horse himself and directed them to mount the other horses, and together they took the piece to Centreville. Its advent was hailed with special delight by every member of the battery. Sergeant Hammond told me that he followed his instructions to the letter; that after directing his cannoneers to serve with the other pieces, he took the piece well to the rear and sought an obscure, and, as he thought, a secure place, and with his drivers remained by it awaiting orders. During the afternoon some cavalry appeared in their near vicinity, and supposing them to be rebel cavalry, they fled, knowing that if they attempted to take the piece with them, it would be captured and they would certainly be taken with it. It is highly probable that the cavalry they saw were a part of our own forces, but such had been the rumors and talk of rebel cavalry, its efficiency and the terrible work it was capable of performing, that the appearance of even a solitary horseman was enough to strike terror to the hearts of half a dozen ordinary men. Sergeant Hammond and his drivers rejoined the company at Centreville, assumed command of his piece, and took it to Washington with the company.*

* This account of the saving of the one piece from capture, does not agree with the statement in Stone's "Rhode Island in the Rebellion," 1864, nor with the "Adjutant General's Report, State of Rhode Island, 1865," which repeats

We reached Fort Runyon about six o'clock in the morning, but no troops were allowed to cross Long Bridge. I remember seeing Colonel Burnside about daylight that morning, pushing forward all alone, considerably in advance of the main column. Occasionally he would stop and look back as if to assure himself that all was right in that direction, as far as it could be right; then he would again push forward. About ten o'clock it became plain that he was looking out for the welfare of his command both in front and rear, for an order was received to allow Colonel Burnside's brigade to cross the bridge, the first who were allowed the privilege of returning to the camps

the statement of Mr. Stone. The testimony of Sergeant Hammond is herewith subjoined, also that of Captain Charles D. Owen:

The account given by Colonel Monroe, of the manner in which was saved from capture one of the pieces of his section, at the first battle of Bull Run, of which piece I was sergeant, is substantially correct.

JOHN H. HAMMOND,
Formerly Sergeant Battery A, First R. I. L. A.,
Late Lieutenant H. G., R. I. V.

To the best of my recollection the account as given by Colonel Monroe is correct.

CHAS. D. OWEN,
Formerly Sergeant Battery A, R. I. L. A.,
Late Captain Battery G, R. I. L. A.

that they had left and which seemed to them like home. In passing through the streets of Washington to our Camp Clark the sidewalks were lined with people, many of whom furnished us with refreshments.

The act of private Scott was finally rewarded by the bestowing upon him a commission as Second Lieutenant, in 1864. The piece was presented by the General Assembly of the State of Rhode Island to Governor Sprague, who placed it in trust with the Providence Marine Corps of Artillery, in whose armory it is now kept.

THIS PAPER WAS READ BEFORE THE RHODE ISLAND SOLDIERS AND SAILORS HISTORICAL SOCIETY, DECEMBER FIRST, 1875.

www.ingramcontent.com/pod-product-compliance
Lightning Source LLC
Chambersburg PA
CBHW021458090426
42739CB00009B/1772